Bilingual Reading Program

Non-fiction
English and Chinese

Community Helpers

社区工作者

By Mei Lan Wang

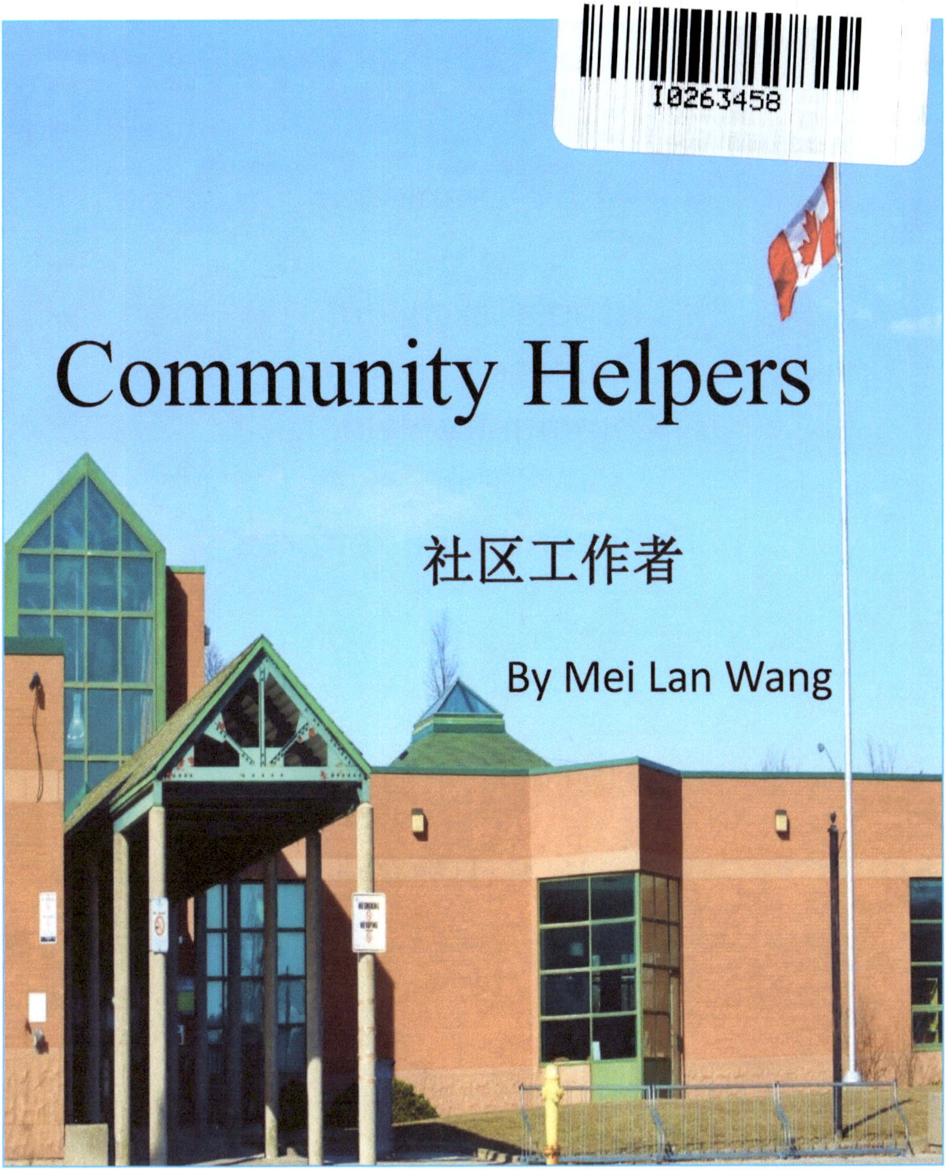

EduOrchids Inc.

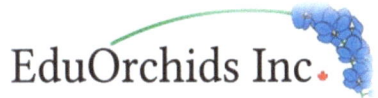

Acknowledgement

A big Thank You
To
Those excellent
Chinese Canadian
Community Helpers
For
Their continuous efforts!

致谢

感谢
这些优秀的
华裔
社区工作者
所作出的不懈努力！

This book is dedicated to
Zhuo and Yue
For their ongoing efforts
To inspire others to learn English!

此书写给
卓和越
感谢他们不懈的努力
鼓励他人学习英语！

Toronto   Xiamen

Community Helpers 社区工作者

Librarian

图书管理员

Community Helpers　社区工作者

Mrs. Li is a **Librarian**.
She helps readers
find the books they need.
She takes good care
of books in the library.

李夫人是**图书管理员**。
她帮助读者
找到他们要找的书。
她精心管理
图书馆里的书籍。

Community Helpers 社区工作者

Nurse

护士

Community Helpers 社区工作者

Yan is a veteran **Nurse**.
She works in a hospital.
Her job is to help patients
to get better soon.

妍是一个经验丰富的**护士**。
她在医院上班。
她的职责是帮助患者
尽快康复。

Community Helpers 社区工作者

General Manager

总经理

Community Helpers　社区工作者

Watson is a **General Manager**. She makes important decisions for her company.

瓦特森
是一家公司的**总经理**。
她负责为公司的运作
做出重要决策。

Community Helpers 社区工作者

Electrician
电工

Community Helpers　社区工作者

Uncle Dong
is an **Electrician**.
He fixes electrical products
for people.
He is also good at
fixing computers.

董叔是个**电工**。
他帮大家修理电器。
他还擅长修理电脑。

Community Helpers   社区工作者

Accountant

会计

Community Helpers 社区工作者

Lillian is an **Accountant**.
She is in charge of
financial records
for her company.

莉莉安是个**会计**。
她主管她公司的
财务出入记录。

Community Helpers 社区工作者

Bookstore Owner

书店老板

Community Helpers　社区工作者

Judith is a
Bookstore Owner.
She sells different kinds
of international magazines.

茱蒂丝是一家**书店老板**。
她代理销售
世界各地的杂志。

Community Helpers　社区工作者

Truck Driver　　卡车司机

Community Helpers　社区工作者

Justin is a **Truck Driver**. He travels all over North America, delivering goods for people.

贾斯汀是个**卡车司机**。
他开着卡车到北美各地
为客户运输货物。

Community Helpers 社区工作者

Chemist

化学实验员

Community Helpers　社区工作者

Ms. Yang is a **Chemist**.
She works in a lab.
She does chemical experiments in her company.

杨女士是个**化学实验员**。
她在实验室里工作。
她在公司
做化学实验。

Community Helpers 社区工作者

Scientist

科学家

Community Helpers 社区工作者

Dr. Wang
is a senior **Scientist**.
Her research focus is on
the trends of climate change
around the world.

王博士是一位
高级科学家。
她的研究重点是
世界气候变化的趋势。

Community Helpers 社区工作者

Insurance Underwriter
保险业务员

Community Helpers 社区工作者

Ying is an **Insurance Underwriter**.
Her job is to process all the insurance claims submitted by their clients.

英是**保险公司业务员**。
她负责处理公司客户
所提交的保险报销业务。

Community Helpers 社区工作者

Ping-pong Coach

乒乓球教练

Community Helpers　社区工作者

Ms. Yang is
a **Ping-pong Coach**.
She coaches Ping-pong at home.
She is also a Ping-pong Referee
in the community.

杨女士是一个**乒乓球教练**。
她在家教人打乒乓球。
她还是社区的乒乓球裁判。

Community Helpers 社区工作者

物流分公司经理

Logistics Branch Manager

Community Helpers　社区工作者

Ms. You is a **Branch Manager** in a logistics company. Her job is to arrange transportation for moving goods around the world.

尤女士是
一个物流**分公司经理**。
她的工作是运输调度，
向世界各地输送物品。

Community Helpers 社区工作者

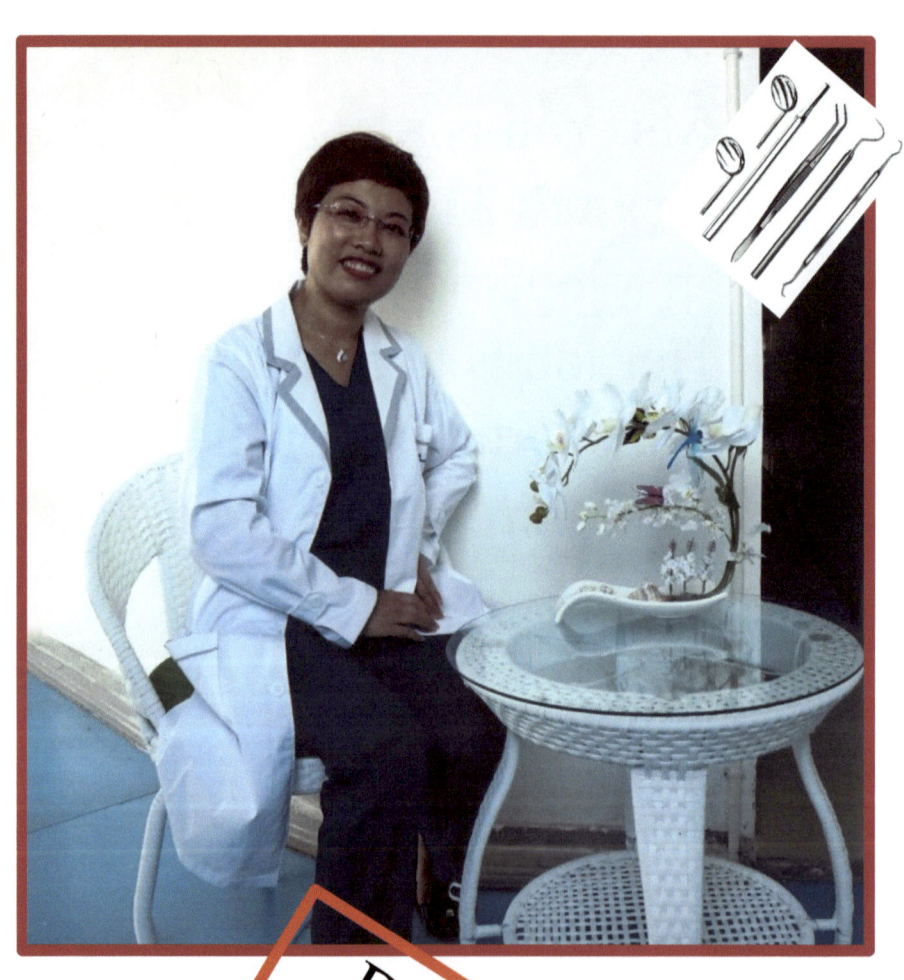

Dentist
牙医

Community Helpers 社区工作者

Dr. Zhou is a **Dentist**.
She takes good care
of her clients' teeth.

周医生是个**牙医**。
她精心护理客户的牙齿。

Community Helpers 社区工作者

Massage Therapist

按摩理疗师

Community Helpers 社区工作者

Shirley is
a **Massage Therapist**.
She helps her clients
to reduce muscular pains
and heal injuries.

索莉是个
按摩理疗师。
她帮助客户减轻肌肉疼痛
及恢复体伤。

Community Helpers　社区工作者

Bus Driver　公交车司机

Community Helpers   社区工作者

Bing is a **Bus Driver**.
His job is to move
people around the city.

炳是**公交车司机**。
他的工作是
送市民到市区的各个目的地。

Community Helpers 社区工作者

Piano Teacher

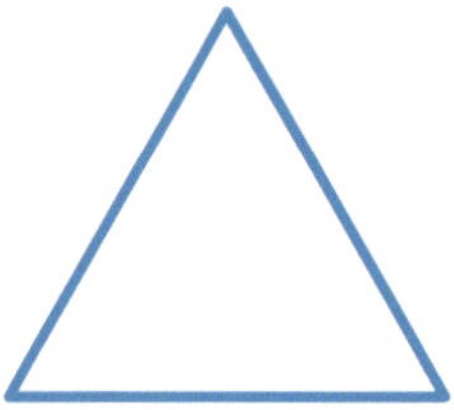

钢琴老师

Community Helpers 社区工作者

Euka is a **Piano Teacher**. She teaches her students how to play the piano. She also helps her clients to select the right piano.

尤佳是个**钢琴老师**。
她教学生弹钢琴。
她还帮客户挑选合适的钢琴。

Community Helpers 社区工作者

Photographer

摄影师

Community Helpers　社区工作者

Mr. Zhang is
a **Photographer**.
He uses his camera to
catch beautiful moments
in the community.

张先生是个**摄影师**。
他用镜头捕捉
社区中的美妙时光。

Community Helpers 社区工作者

Special Education Teacher
特殊教育老师

Community Helpers   社区工作者

Mei is a
Special Education Teacher.
She provides direct in-class
support for students with
special needs.

梅是个特殊教育老师。
她为有特殊需求的学生
提供课堂直接辅助。

Community Helpers 社区工作者

Retired Farmer

退休农民

Community Helpers　社区工作者

Mama Wu is a **Retired Farmer**.
She likes to help around.
She enjoys watering
the flowers and vegetables.

吴妈妈是个**退休农民**。
她喜欢帮忙干活。
浇花草蔬菜是她的乐趣。

Community Helpers 社区工作者

Future Community Helper
未来的社区工作者

Community Helpers 社区工作者

Baby Zhuang is a **Future Community Helper**.
She is keen on practising doodling on paper.
She is well-prepared for school.

庄宝宝是**未来的社区工作者**。
她专心致志,练习纸上涂鸦。
她已做好上学的准备。

Vocabulary	词汇
Accountant 会计	Logistics Branch Manager 运输分公司经理
Bookstore Owner 书店老板	Massage Therapist 按摩理疗师
Bus Driver 公交车司机	Nurse 护士
Chemist 化学实验员	Photographer 摄影师
Dentist 牙医	Piano Teacher 钢琴老师
Electrician 电工	Ping-pong Coach 乒乓球教练
Future Community Helper 未来社区工作者	Retired Farmer 退休农民
General Manager 总经理	Scientist 科学家
Insurance Underwriter 保险业务员	Special Education Teacher 特殊教育老师
Librarian 图书管理员	Truck Driver 卡车司机

Non-fiction Photo Story
Bilingual Reading Program
For Grades K-3
English and Chinese Vocabulary

Text copyright @2020 by Mei Lan Wang
All rights reserved.
Published by EduOrchids Inc., Canada
Bilingual Reading Program
First Printed in April, 2020

ISBN: 978-1999-2858-38

EduOrchids Inc.

USD $10.99 CAD $ 15.99

www.ingramcontent.com/pod-product-compliance
Lightning Source LLC
Chambersburg PA
CBHW041822040426
42453CB00005B/130